CHRISTINE GREGORY

I CAN BE A MIRROR

MY ROLE IN MISSION ACTION AND PERSONAL WITNESSING

Study Guide by Lynn Yarbrough

This book is the text for a course in the study area Missions of the Church Study Course.

Published by Woman's Missionary Union, Auxiliary to Southern Baptist Convention, P. O. Box C-10, Birmingham, Alabama 35283-0010: Marjorie J. McCullough, president; Carolyn Weatherford, executive director; Bobbie Sorrill, associate executive director, Missions Education System; Lynn Yarbrough, Publications Section director; Karen C. Simons, Products Group manager.

Deena W. Newman, editor
Cathy D. Butler, editor
Janell E. Young, artist
Kathryne Solomon, editorial assistant

Woman's Missionary Union
Birmingham, Alabama

©1987 by Woman's Missionary Union
All rights reserved. Published 1988.
Printed in the United States of America.

Library of Congress Cataloging-in-Publication Data

Gregory, Christine, 1921-
  I can be a mirror.

  1. Witness bearing (Christianity) 2. Evangelistic work. 3. Women—Religious life. I. Yarbrough, Lynn. II. Title.
BV4527.G74   1988   248'.5   88-10742
ISBN 0-936625-23-6

W883107 • 8M • 0488

CONTENTS

INTRODUCTION

"Whatever you have done unto the least of these, you have done unto me." Like a bell in an empty room, the words echo round and round the churches of America.

Yet, knowing where to start in following the command of Jesus presents an awesome challenge in today's world— a challenge, but not an obstacle.

Mission action involves ministering and witnessing to persons of special need and circumstance who are not members of the church or its programs. Personal witnessing is a Christian's sharing the gospel of Jesus Christ with another person and giving that person an opportunity to confess Jesus Christ as Saviour and Lord.

Ministering is necessary and witnessing essential. By combining these two actions into one function, we fulfill Christ's command to go to all people to tell the good news of salvation. Planting a witness as one ministers can explain *why* you are there, *why* people care; telling *what* God has done for you; sharing *who* Jesus is.

We live in a world where there is more lostness than ever before. As followers of Christ we step into the world with the question of *how* on our lips and in our hearts. We know we have *the* answer so the question becomes one of methodology and motivation.

Motivation is one of the most important and widely used words in the English vocabulary. From the largest business corporations to any two-person relationship, our minds, either consciously or subconsciously, are trying to think up ways we can get other people to do the things we want them to do. Some of these motives are self-serving; some are altruistic; some are both. Mission action and personal witnessing are surely the latter. We are motivated by obedience to God. An added benefit is personal satisfaction, for what brings more joy to the Christian than seeing another find the Saviour?

It is my unabashed hope that I can motivate people to become involved in the Master's plan, ministering and witnessing to the Master's world. By examples of the ministries of others and through the motivational words of authors from Genesis through the twentieth century, may both writer and reader be inspired to follow the commandment of Jesus to love others as we were loved by Him. For He said, "If you have love one for another, then everyone will know that you are my disciples" (John 13:35 TEV).

To that end this book is a composite of the work of many others.

WMU defines *mission action* as ministering and witnessing to persons of special need or circumstance who are not members of the church or its programs; mission action is also combating social and moral problems.

WMU defines *personal witnessing* as a Christian's sharing the gospel of Jesus Christ with another person and giving that person an opportunity to confess Jesus Christ as Saviour and Lord.

Are You Ready for Mission Action?—A Checkup

1. Do you genuinely want to find Christ's will for your life as it relates to your personal ministry?

2. Do you come from a socioeconomic background which makes it very painful for you to work with persons of similar background? Or, did that preparation make it easy for you to reach out to persons who have similar needs?

3. Are you prejudiced? Come on now; be honest. This will help you in overcoming some barriers. A young school teacher said, "I was never prejudiced toward anyone, I thought, until I realized that I could have a child who had AIDS in my classroom."

4. Are you willing to be a servant? Jesus was the supreme servant and He instructed us to take on the same attitude.

5. Why do you want to minister?

6. Do you just want to offer help or do you need help yourself?

PART I

I Can Do Mission Action

1
I Can Live Out My Commitment to Jesus

Two truths have emerged with crystal clearness in the thinking of twentieth-century Christians. One is the worth of the individual. Jesus taught it and since the Resurrection it has slowly, but surely, become a part of the spiritual wealth of mankind. The second is that a person is a social being created by God to live in fellowship with the Creator and responsibly with his or her fellow human beings.

If we read the New Testament, we shall see that the method of the gospel is not social reform on a mass scale, but Jesus redeeming individuals and sending them back to their communities to witness for Him. They had been given hope; they were now to give it to others. Paul gave the injunction, "Keep on working with fear and trembling to complete your salvation, because God is always at work in you to make you willing and able to obey his own purpose" (Phil. 2:12-13 TEV).

Southern Baptists really want their mission to be making individuals whole in Christ Jesus. The Baptist Faith and Message was first adopted by the Southern Baptist Convention in 1925.

Article XV of the Baptist Faith and Message, the statements of Christian faith commonly held among Southern Baptists, strongly speaks to the Christian's responsibility in the social order. Three specific areas are mentioned:

1

"The Christian should oppose in the spirit of Christ every form of greed, selfishness, and vice.

"He should work to provide for the orphaned, the needy, the aged, the helpless, and the sick.

"Every Christian should seek to bring industry, government, and society as a whole under the sway of the principles of righteousness, truth, and brotherly love."

In summary, it is a charge to offer hope in the saving grace of Jesus and hope that man can be made whole.

Mission action is a program designed to minister and witness to persons of special need and circumstances who, without this special effort, are often bypassed in the church's direct outreach activities. It is not just doing good. Through mission action women minister in such a way that the person being helped is confronted with the unmistakable truth that God's people care because God cares. He cares enough that He sent His Son to die so that one person could be whole.

Mission action is an answer to questions many Christian women are asking themselves: How is God calling me to live out my Christian commitment? Where can I find my niche in alleviating some of the hurting in this world? How can I use my spiritual gifts to bring people to my Jesus?

Mission action has always been a part of the work of Woman's Missionary Union. It has not always been called by that name, but from the earliest years WMU leaders have believed that part of the "laborers for the harvest" were Woman's Missionary Union's own members.

In an address soon after she became the WMU president in 1906, Fannie E. S. Heck said: "In the truest sense the field of the Union is in the hearts of Southern Baptist women and children. This field must supply the seed that by and by shall give the Bread of Life to hungering multitudes in destitute quarters of their own and other lands."

Woman's Missionary Union policy in 1910-11 initiated a new movement known as Personal Service. The purpose? To bring hope to communities through volunteer Christian witness in such activities as mother's meetings, sewing schools, mission Sunday Schools, visitation to the sick and prisoners. The groundwork had been laid in Baltimore by the multifaceted work of Annie Armstrong as she worked

2

with immigrants, the shelter for destitute children, and the Ladies Bay View Mission to the Bay View Asylum. Annually about 2,500 persons were admitted to the asylum. They were generally between the ages of 20 and 50, diseased, addicted to alcohol, and in some cases insane. Annie Armstrong was a leader in showing women how they could bring the hope that God intended for all to those of little hope.

The first *Manual of Personal Service,* written by Fannie Heck and Emma Leachman, was an increasing emphasis on deep personal involvement. The manual led women to establish settlement houses. Later the houses became known as Good Will Centers and took the motto, Peace on Earth, Good Will Toward Men. They began to examine their community needs.

The rise of young children employed in factories in the early 1900s led to the Federal Child Labor Law. Women used their influence to see that their state's laws were concurrent with the national law.

In the context of personal service, women were urged to conduct Daily Vacation Bible Schools for the 20 million children in the summer months when schools were closed. Literacy work began in 1922 because committed Baptist women saw the awful handicap under which illiterate adults labored.

All my life I have been the beneficiary of the models of Baptist Women doing personal service. It was through the personal service of my own mother that I gained my first appreciation for ministry outside the normal reaches of the church. She did her personal service with blacks in an adjoining community. In the Great Depression years of the 1920s, my mother's concern was not only that they have the necessities of life, but the joys, those things which brought strong self-images and hope for the future, though the present then looked very bleak. I can, 60 years later, almost smell the cold wood ashes in a potbellied stove in a black church building where we sat on a straight plank bench while she taught them hymns and Scripture verses. Later in our own home, she strived to teach them sewing and cooking, although she was far from a pro in either field.

In 1942 the name *personal service* was changed to *community missions*. (Is it possible that something was lost in the transition?) Women and girls were challenged to work in their communities to magnify Christ.

Mission action was introduced in 1965 to emphasize the intensified witnessing and ministering approach to community missions. Since that time, thorough and detailed materials have been written for every age level in the church. Readers are urged to find those who are outside the church membership who need love and care.

Ruth Wagner Miller, author of *The Mission Action Book,* gave a good answer to the question, Why do mission action? She said, "We need to eat, sleep, breathe, and exercise in order to have a healthy physical body. We need to eat (study God's Word), sleep (rest in the Lord), breathe (be filled with the Holy Spirit), and exercise (serve others), for the spiritual health of ourselves and every other member of the body of Christ. Mission action is what we do—our exercise."

Hence, to be involved in mission action is to become an aggressive advocate of a saving gospel and all moral and social righteousness.

As we study the four Gospels, we find over and over and over that the good news brought salvation and salvation in turn brought concern about what we would do. The Gospel of Luke is one example. In Luke, the immediate question was, What do we do in response to salvation and repentance?

As John preached in the territory of the Jordan River and crowds were baptized, they asked, "What are we to do?" And John said, "Whoever has two shirts must give one to the man who has none, and whoever has food must share it" (Luke 3:10-11 TEV). Tax collectors were told, "Don't collect any more than is legal." Soldiers were told, "Don't accuse anyone falsely."

Then Jesus came! Into His teachings went practice! He cast out demons; He healed many diseases—skin, fever, paralysis, the woman with the issue of blood, people with evil spirits. He raised the dead and He fed the hungry. He moved into every facet of the lives of people of His time

4

and He showed them that He was indeed the Son of God. Then He said, "You are witnesses of these things."

Our task is to continue to show people that Jesus was God Who became human that we might better understand the nature of God. He made life worthwhile.

John emphasizes the how of our discipleship when he writes "Love one another. As I have loved you, so you must love one another. If you have love for one another, then everyone will know that you are my disciples (John 13:34-35 TEV)."

Matthew shows that Christian discipleship conforms to the law. He records Jesus saying that man must love God with his total being and his neighbor as much as he loves himself. This was the fulcrum of the law.

Over and over Old Testament prophets had chastised Israel for wandering away from God and following false gods. When they strayed from God they also neglected their responsibility to look after the poor and hungry, care for the widowed and orphans, welcome the stranger, and extend justice to all.

The religious leaders of Jesus' day were warned that if they did not conform to the standards of God's kingdom, the mission of being His redemptive instrument would be taken from them and would be given to those who would believe, follow, and accept the mission.

Now, I am personally assigned the responsibility to mirror God's nature to my neighbors. God is love and if I am to be like Him, I must follow His example.

This Is the Big Question

Does the claim that you know Jesus Christ make a difference in your life Monday through Saturday—in use of time, money, strength, and in your value system?

2
I Can Do Mission Action Alone

Ellen Davis is a smart, sophisticated Baptist woman who is highly energetic and devoted to all missions causes. Because she is of a generation of women who are activity-oriented, she enjoys being involved in some project.

She serves breakfast every Sunday morning to hungry, homeless people, mostly men, but occasionally women. Summer and winter, spring and fall, Ellen rolls out of bed in her lovely home in an affluent neighborhood, and is at the church by 6:30. Perking the coffee, frying eggs and bacon, and pouring juice are all joyful tasks to her. When the first hungry person arrives, she greets him or her as she would a guest in her own home.

Recently she said, "Those men ate (she had served 20 that morning) as if they had never seen food before!"

A devotional and prayertime follows breakfast. The guests are warmly invited to Sunday School and worship and Ellen is off to another area of the church spreading sunshine.

Ellen is a motivator too. Business people who witness to colleagues and business acquaintances have encouraged reluctant prospects to come to Ellen's Sunday morning breakfast. Recently, one of those fellows came and later joined the church. Dressed in clean overalls and weeping tears of repentance, he had found his way once again. There were tears of joy in the congregation that day too!

Nurine Wright is a beautiful, blond-haired, blue-eyed Baptist young woman. She is recognized immediately as a leader. The chaplain for a hospital for terminally ill children began taking Nurine with him to the hospital to visit these little ones. Nurine saw a need.

Families of these hospitalized children are allowed to bring younger family members to visit. It was apparent that the young visitors did not know how to communicate with the ill sibling for long periods of time, or the ill child was not up to long visits.

Nurine offered to entertain these active children while parents visited with the patient. Crayons, games, books, and stories are her tool of mission action. Two or three evenings a week she goes to the hospital with her sunshine.

This kind of attention does not have to be confined to hospitals. Many of us have friends who need free time from children and elderly parents. Being separated from them just a few hours brings rest and refreshment both to the caretaker and her charges.

Lorene Goodson is known worldwide for her aprons and potholders. She is known in Calhoun City, Mississippi, as the woman who bakes birthday cakes for all of the county prisoners. And, when they work the area around her house, she is not afraid. She calls in some friends and they prepare lunch for the prisoners. "I was in prison and you came unto me." Lorene Goodson did.

Alma Hunt, the retired executive director of WMU, SBC, performs a most unusual ministry in time of bereavement. She visits the family home, the funeral home, and takes her tape recorder to the funeral.

Later she sits down and writes beautiful letters to absent family members and friends. The careful details which she supplies are relished with tears and thanksgiving by those who have felt estranged because they could not be present. Indeed these letters draw persons closer to God and to each other.

Alma would function well with my friend Mary Stuart Sodergren who goes into the home of the bereaved at the

7

appropriate time and gathers and polishes the shoes of family members. Dressing for the funeral is one step easier. She does what she can.

Every mother has the potential for witnessing and ministering right at her doorstep. Almost every week I hear friends talk about the peer groups of their children in terms of latchkey children, children of single parents, and husbands and fathers who must be away much of each week working. The strong Christian family frequently finds itself in the role of surrogate family and substitute fathers and mothers.

Opportunities to minister and witness come at unexpected times. Several times I have not wanted to attend a business dinner. My frustration over having to attend has soon been forgotten when the dinner partner I most feared dropped his facade long enough to divulge his deep hurts and needs. I know now he did it because of who he thought I was. The opportunity for witness was at that very moment; in all likelihood I would never see him again.

Jesus protected the shy and quiet among us. He knew that all need to minister but some would prefer to keep it quiet. Matthew 6:2 reads, "Make certain you do not perform your religious duties in public so that people will see what you do."

Sometimes it seems we have no real way to reach the hurting one—one whose baby was born out of wedlock, the alienated child, the partner in a broken marriage.

"She cried and shared with me how she held the beautiful little grandson in her arms and loved him before they gave him up for adoption."

"I am going to have a baby and I am not married. I am going to keep my baby and tell him all about his daddy."

"We are going to be living apart." You've heard this and deep, deep down you knew that their living apart began with living apart from God many years back. Yet life goes on. In the midst of the tears we know that these are God-given chances to minister and witness one-on-one.

8

Two teenage boys ran away from seemingly loving, affluent homes. Two fathers responded to anxiety and fear differently.

One father said, "When he comes back I am going to beat him until he can't move."

His neighbor said, "I am going to put my arms around him and look him in the eye and say, 'Randy, I love you so much!' "

Randy's mother prayed, "O God, bring them home safely and we, like You, will give them another chance."

Her body trembled with rage and fright as she talked about her beloved child, the one for whom she had dreamed and planned. How could a daughter just walk away? How could she turn from a home where love abounded and go with someone who lied and cheated and had nothing?

Oh the hurts and the need for ministry. Why do we think we have to have the answers? Why can't we just reach out or go and say, "I know you are hurting and I want you to know that I care deeply. There is One Who is stronger than I Who not only promised to bear those awful burdens, He also promised to go with us if we go in His name to minister."

Hardly a day passes that we do not hear of some need that a lone woman could answer—in prayer, in the offer of friendship, in putting strong arms around the weak. And she does it in the name of Jesus.

This Is the Big Question
You are frustrated because "they" won't do anything. After reading some ideas from this book, choose a way that you can do mission action outside the normal reaches of your church.

3
I Can Minister and Witness to the Hungry and Poor

Thanksgiving is a joyous time for many Americans. As families and friends gather and enjoy a national holiday, there is too much food, too much football, and too much forgetting of those who have not.

In a recent year, a week before Thanksgiving, school children in the United States were urged to give up their lunch to help some starving child elsewhere have something to eat. This emotional appeal made children think that somehow by such admirable sacrifice, peanut butter and jelly sandwiches could go from pink and blue lunchboxes to hungry youngsters in Ethiopia, Mali, Puerto Rico, or even Chicago.

Most people in parts of the world where food is unobtainable eat rice, wheat, corn, sorghum, carsava, or potatoes; not peanut butter, beef, pork, or poultry. Poor people cannot get to what is available. When they can find food, they cannot afford to buy it, even when three-quarters of their disposable income is spent on food. In the early 1980s we learned that transportation was a number one problem in feeding people.

During 1982 people in one part of Zimbabwe lined up for hours to receive a pitiful dole of cornmeal while in

10

another part of the country there was a cornmeal surplus. A philanthropic organization underwrote the cost of moving the meal from one part of the country to the other. Concerned outsiders determined that as much as Ethiopia needed food, it needed trucks and light airplanes to deliver the supplies to where there was a desperate need. The Southern Baptist Foreign Mission Board responded to the need of the over-the-mountain roads by furnishing a roadgrader.

Robert Parham, director of Hunger Concerns for the Christian Life Commission of the Southern Baptist Convention, has done much to keep the facts and figures before Southern Baptists.

Statistics often are ignored until they relate to our own area. When I read that infant mortality rates and the rate of children living in poverty in the Bible Belt are indications of the brutal force of poverty in America, I immediately think, "That's my territory." Of course, when infants and children are victims, so are their families.

An Alabama mother of two anemic preschool children told a team investigating hunger in America, "We're doing OK, just ain't got no food."

Persons living on retirement incomes (mostly just meager Social Security or pensions) could frequently voice similar statements. Often too proud or too uninformed to let their needs be known, these hidden people are abused by the system. To ask for community help or food stamps would be saying, "I am a failure. I didn't work hard enough." We have not told them clearly, "You are important! Sales tax on food, continuing inadequate financial assistance, and Social Security and pensions based on very lean earnings make you the victim! We want to help you."

Mission action-interested persons can have clear-cut, definitive plans in action for feeding the hungry and assisting the elderly.

On a morning when the thermometer stood at 15° F at noon, I gathered up all the warm clothing I could find and carried it to the Salvation Army. Their soup kitchen was in full swing and over 100 people would sit down together to have their only meal of the day and to get really warm for a brief time. A mission action group *could* serve that meal.

Yet, for the 100 there would 400 or 500 more who could not get to the Salvation Army building.

Mission action would say that several churches could join together and for at least two or three days in the week offer soup and bread (most bakers are willing to donate day-old bread) in different sections of a city or town. People talk and listen easily when they come into "warm" relationships. Then it is easy to talk about the love of God.

While some persons are feeding people in churches, others may take the same kind of food to the elderly and ill who are homebound. Social agencies are more than willing to provide names. These meals provide an entree into homes where more than physical food is needed. Only those who love should be in these projects for it takes much loving to overlook some of the conditions (it might also involve some laundry and housecleaning).

Gathering food for distribution is an excellent associational WMU or church WMU project. At one time I knew of a rural church that had an overstocked family crisis pantry and no one came to use it. Had they been in an association where food collection was done jointly by all interested persons then mission action groups could have taken the food, sorted it into family-size grocery bags, and taken it where it was needed. Remember that wherever food is given in the name of mission action, there must be personal contact made by the Christian church persons. To share the love of Christ by our actions and words is the good of missons.

Parham has written, "The silence and noninvolvement of churches in public policy advocation on domestic hunger contributes to the state of the South's poverty and hunger-stricken children. The churches generously open their pantries to the needy and shy away from openly initiating and supporting responsible public policy."

A letter-writing campaign urging congressmen to support antihunger legislation will encourage them to use this country's vast resources to feed hungry people. It is not a call for a donation but for Christian action.

As much as $40,000,000 per year is spent by lobbyists trying to influence Congress. The churches of the Southern Baptist Convention do not have that kind of money available. Its sources of strength are people and the power of the Lord Jesus Christ. Money is never a substitute for personal involvement.

"Simon, son of John, do you love me more than these others do?"

"Yes, Lord," he answered, "You know that I love You."

Jesus said to him, "Take care of my lambs." Three times in John 21:15-17 Jesus asked Peter if he loved him and three times in hearing Peter's affirmative answer, Jesus said, "Take care of my lambs."

Jesus calls every Christian by name and the directive is the same, "Take care of my lambs."

On the local level many Southern Baptist churches such as the Calvary Baptist Church in Roanoke, Virginia, have a way of ministering to the immediate community. On the six Wednesday nights prior to Easter, they have rice meals instead of a traditional Wednesday night supper. The cost of the meal is the same as usual, $2.00 to $2.25. Rice is served and the remainder of the money goes to community hunger.

Other churches have specific days for bringing specific items. For example, on one Sunday everyone brings flour, on another dried milk, and on another dried fruit or beans. In one church I saw Royal Ambassadors putting jars of peanut butter in a wheelbarrow. A wheelbarrow full of jars of peanut butter was a sight long to be remembered! All of these foods were stacked into the church's food pantry to fill needs as they arise. Local individuals in need can benefit from this person-to-person ministry.

Once a group of us decided to buy a week's groceries for a family of four. When we learned that food stamps do not cover detergents and cleaning supplies such as mops and brooms, we added those to our grocery list. Then a member volunteered to do the shopping. She exhibited a beautiful Christian spirit; she bought the biggest sizes and the best brands (not always necessarily name brands). Then she bought extra snacks with her own money. She reminded me of another friend who years before said, "Don't cut off the pretty buttons before you give a coat to the needy."

We need to be constantly aware of food surpluses. We can make surpluses available to people who can use them and can furnish transportation for moving them. For example, a Methodist minister discovered that potatoes were left behind after harvesters went through the fields. He arranged for them to be picked up and trucked to the needy.

To feed the hungry is to live life-styles which show that Baptist women manage the resources of God's world with compassion and fairness. Jesus outlined our priorities. In His teaching about the faithful servant, Jesus said, "Much is required of the person to whom much more is given" (Luke 12:48 TEV).

The life-styles of the early Christians clearly showed they understood Jesus' teaching. He had told the rich young ruler to sell all he had and to give it to the poor. The young ruler failed. Early Christians did not.

"The group of believers was of one mind and heart. No one said that any of his belongings was his own, but they all shared with one another everything they had. . . . There was no one in the group who was in need. Those who owned fields or houses would sell them, bring the money received from the sale, and turn it over to the apostles; and the money was distributed to each one according to his need" (Acts 4:32, 34-35 TEV).

How could they do this? The secret is in verse 33 of Acts 4: "With great power the apostles gave witness to the resurrection of the Lord Jesus, and God poured rich blessings on them all."

To feed the hungry is to pray for the power to act in love. What individuals cannot do alone can be done by the church. What the church cannot do alone can be done by groups of churches. A retired couple in New York acted by preserving surplus fruits from their area during the summer and early fall. Their fruits became part of what their church did to assist in a community effort during the hard winter months. What would happen if Baptist women came together with surpluses from their gardens on summer days and made soups for freezing? In cold weather it could go to the needy or it might furnish a soup kitchen for the hungry.

Ruth Miller wrote, "A Christian who accumulates wealth chooses wealth as the home for her heart. A Christian who acts in love toward God and neighbor chooses love as the home for her heart."

The Ministry/Witness Resource Guide, *Domestic Hunger,* brings Baptist leaders face-to-face with some of the misconceptions we hold about hunger in the United States. For example, it has long been assumed that dark-skinned people constitute the larger percentage of the poor, while, in fact, two-thirds of all poor people are white. We have assumed that if you have a job and earn at least minimum wages, you can survive. The fact is that a worker earning a wage of $3.35 an hour and working fulltime receives an annual salary which is only 65 percent of the poverty level. We have wrongly assumed that a person is poor because he is lazy. Poor job skills, illiteracy, bad health; and the high cost of childcare, transportation, clothing, and food are among the reasons which prevent the needy from seeking help and jobs.

As women, we should note that two out of three adults who are poor are women. Fifty percent of all poor families are headed by women. They also have the highest rate of unemployment and earn $.69 for every $1.00 earned by men. These women are very often untrained, functionally illiterate, and desperately in need of help in planning ways to educate and better themselves.

Missions organizations have available resources if members are willing to be God's servants. Three programs can be found in nearly every community: (1) Special Supplemental Food Program for Women, Infants, and Children (WIC—Department of Agriculture), a program to provide supplemental foods and nutrition education through local agencies to eligible people. (2) Headstart, a comprehensive health, educational, nutritional, and social program to economically disadvantaged preschool children and their families. (3) Public schools, which offer opportunities for

15

volunteer services in tutoring, special education, nursing, and adult education. On a professional basis, evening classes and training opportunities are offered to parents. These are only a few of the resources available to God's servants.

As mentioned in chapter 7, mission action is both preventive and corrective. Adults are helped to correct their self-image and improve their skills while the child is helped to prevent the same problems from occurring generation after generation. The afternoon tutoring programs in a number of the churches in our city have greatly advanced the learning abilities and self-confidence of numerous children. Since a father figure is absent in so many of their homes, a male tutor (a retired man, a church staff member, the associational director of missions) has been an outstanding asset.

To quote the ministry/witness resource guide: "The reality of poverty, hunger, and suffering in the richest nation of the world should shock and motivate us to mission action."

This Is the Big Question

Write one thing you will covenant with God to do to relieve hunger in your community. It could be a plan of action for your missions organizations.

4
I Can Minister and Witness to the Prisoner

She was 16 years old. She looked at the iron bars on the windows of the red brick buildings. Her eyes fell on the ten-foot-high chainlink fence which surrounded the building. The fence was topped with razor-sharp barbed wire. For the next 12 years, the North Carolina Correctional Center for Women in Raleigh, North Carolina, would be her home.

She would live with approximately 550 other women; 60 percent would be under 20 years of age; most would be high school dropouts; three-fourths would have children; 17 percent would not be married but would be the primary caretakers of those children. The majority listed their denominational affiliation as Baptist.

An ugly, stark picture, isn't it? Surely not the proper setting for Baptist women.

Yet a group of Baptist Young Women didn't believe that and wrote to the Woman's Missionary Union of North Carolina asking, "What can we do?"

That question was to revitalize a program that North Carolina WMU had begun in 1966. Three halfway houses in North Carolina, at Raleigh, North Wilkesboro, and Lumberton, received the loving, caring affirmation of Baptist women. These women had responded to the request of the central correctional institution to help honor-grade prisoners make a re-entry into society. They hoped the women who had been incarcerated would be able to find friends, housing, and a job in their own communities while still under the jurisdiction of correctional officials.

With the change of administrators this program was abandoned. Not until the early 1970s were volunteers welcomed again.

One very cold day, Nona Bickerstaff, a member of the North Carolina WMU staff, was waiting at the gate of the correctional center. She noticed that a female inmate standing nearby was wearing only a light sweater. Nona talked with the woman and discovered she did not own a coat. Almost immediately North Carolina WMU purchased a coat for her and large-sized clothing for another inmate who needed it badly.

These were small beginnings, but they gained the attention and confidence of the correctional staff. The correctional staff began to call the North Carolina WMU office for other needs—tape recorders for each dorm, the entire Bible on tape for a woman in solitary confinement, clothing, and even a punching bag to help relieve hostility and frustration.

At the beginning only the state WMU staff had been consistently involved. Then someone else had an idea: Every woman in prison should have a Christmas present. The help of the associational WMU was solicited. Would women give toothbrushes, toothpaste, lotions, lipsticks, and other articles approved by the institution? They could, and they would!

The first year the gifts were put in sacks. Then the association made large Christmas stockings. Another year, more than 600 women received tube socks, scarves, gloves, nice soap, and lovely Christmas cards. The gifts were placed in the prettiest Christmas boxes that could be bought. It was a tremendous mission action project. It was a continuing way for Baptist women to prove their trustworthiness. The Scripture portions in each box told the story of Christ's love. The women who gave enacted it. Women entered the lives of the prisoners in an indirect way. They could not go in, so they sent.

18

The second "big" idea came when someone asked, "Why don't we have a retreat for the honor-grade offenders?" Mundo Vista was the perfect place. The North Carolina WMU camp facility was away from large centers of population; it had a seven-foot-high fence all around it with an electronically controlled gate; and it was in a beautiful wooded area.

The proposal was made to prison officials, a miracle took place, and permission was granted.

The first retreat was for long-term offenders. WMU leaders believe the Long-termer's Retreat is the only time the State Department of Corrections allows the inmates not approved for home leave to be away from the prison for overnight occasions.

Now two retreats are held each year. One for youthful offenders (remember the 16-year-old?) is held on a weekend during the regular summer camp program and is staffed by the same summer staff. The program is essentially the same, even to a missionary speaker.

In the fall, older women come just prior to the meeting of North Carolina WMU Executive Board. Executive Board members and other women volunteers form the staff. Of course, at first everyone is insecure and frightened, but soon they relax and feel comfortable. An abundance of good food, a good program, and warm friendliness soon make the inmates feel loved and welcomed. The correctional facility is responsible for security.

Nancy Curtis of North Carolina WMU says, "It is a life-changing experience for both groups!"

Several years ago, women across the state spent thousands of dollars to provide bedspreads, coordinating towels, and washcloths for each dorm room at the correctional institution. Another year the special gift was to provide curtains for the dorm rooms and draperies for the living/lounge rooms.

Several years ago, women across the state spent thousands of dollars to provide bedspreads, coordinating towels, and washcloths for each dorm room at the correctional institution. Another year the special gift was to provide curtains for the dorm rooms and draperies for the living/

lounge rooms. Thus, women supported those doing mission action.

Nancy says, "This was a headache to accomplish, but fun!"

Nancy feels that the forgotten groups are the families of inmates and the prison staff. She has suggested ways Baptist women can minister and witness to them.

Women all over North Carolina continued to be involved with these prison women. Some have followed them back into the prisoner's home environment, offering encouragement, helping them to find jobs and a better way of life.

Wherever there are prisoners there are also families back somewhere. Whatever the cause for incarceration, there is still the bond of family ties. On an occasion several years ago when the chaplain of the women's prison in my state called and asked if I would bring two young children to see their mother, I said, "Sure!" thinking that this would be an easy sort of mission action. But, when I saw the meeting of that mother with those children, it was the most heartrending experience I ever felt. She had committed awful deeds against them; yet, she was still their mother.

The loss of a father in the home can place untold burdens both emotionally and financially upon the family. Mission action ministers!

Because of the great social stigma attached, families often withdraw both from society and from the inmate. Reach out and minister to them. Churches may become involved by training a court watcher who sits in on court cases to determine who needs ministry.

Go to your jail, county prison units, and state incarceration facilities and ask what you may do as a volunteer.

This Is the Big Question

Reading material and recreational equipment (games, etc.) arc always in short supply in any incarceration unit. Would you be willing to take these and Scripture portions to the nearest unit? Did you ever think of asking to teach a literacy class in a prison?

5
I Can Minister and Witness to Migrants

I was 20 years old when I had my first encounter with migrants through Vacation Bible School. Their pathos called forth an emotion in me that I still have 45 years later. They were few in my part of the country then, but with the mobility of society and the decreasing size of farm families, they are more and more numerous. The Home Mission Board reports that there are more east-west migrations now than were previously seen. In the semi-rural area in which I now live, one rarely saw migrants 10 years ago; now they come in large numbers to harvest tobacco and other farm crops.

Migrants live on the farms and are almost hidden until Saturday when they come to the supermarkets to do their shopping. I was almost unaware of them until I did my grocery shopping one Saturday morning. In passing the spice shelf, I saw a dark-skinned man opening spice boxes. He licked his finger, put it into the box, and put it back into his mouth. Immediately I knew he was looking for chili powder and couldn't read the labels! I simply reached for the chili powder and put it in his hands. Again my heart felt that tug.

A young Cuban-born woman in our church began a Sunday afternoon Bible class for migrants. Women of area churches made cookies. For a few hours on Sunday this became a ministry to those outside the normal reaches of the church.

The Baptist church at Beaufort, South Carolina, has a 25-year-old ministry to migrants which developed as a result of a mission study. Mrs. Ashley Graves was challenged by W. C. Fields's book *The Chains Are Strong*. This is her story.

"In 1963, as WMU president (now called WMU director) at the Baptist church at Beaufort, it was my privilege to be a part of a relay team teaching the Home Mission Study, *The Chains Are Strong*. My chapter was "Prisons Without Walls." As I studied and prepared to teach, my thoughts kept coming back to the words of Rev. J. Ed Taylor, Home Mission Board missionary to the migrants in Pharr, Texas: 'They are the waifs and strays of the working world, imprisoned by a wall-less vagabondage which leaves them way-worn and travel-stained. And so it goes, year after year. The children grow up; the parents get older. And if someone does not provide an opportunity, such a family never knows the warmth and encouragement which Christian friends can supply. Thousands spend their lives in the nomadic fashion and die without knowing Christ as Saviour. And they live right here in Christian America!'

"The words of Gerald Palmer, (then) associate Home Mission Board Language Group ministries director, haunted my mind, 'The first essential is heartfelt interest in every individual regardless of his economic or social condition. All the promotion that our agencies and missionaries can give will never be effective until some individual in a local church gets this matter on his heart and decides to do something about it.'

"The burden for migrant people was on my heart. So intense was my feeling that it came through to the 35 women who were meeting in a home here on Lady Island that night. After the study, we fell on our knees and asked God's direction and leadership. They asked me to talk with our pastor.

"Dr. George A. Jones contacted J. Ed Taylor who was then missionary to the migrants on the East Coast and Florida.

"Brother Taylor came and spoke to our (then) Woman's Missionary Society in April that year. He so challenged our hearts that we knew God was leading us to begin a ministry to the migrants.

"It was not easy in 1963. There were so many objections in business meetings, etc. But God was leading and, praise His Holy name, the motion carried and we were able to use the church (sanctuary) and education buildings.

"As we began the ministry, Rev. and Mrs. Taylor came and spent the month of June with us that year. In early May, we began a clothing drive and began to make health kits. We located and visited the (migrant) camps. A few of us, that is! We had no funding but we had the strong conviction of the leadership of the Holy Spirit.

"We found some 3,500 migrants in our county that first year. Many families of 10 or 12 were living in one room— beautiful children with big black eyes and curly hair. Many spoke no English but there was always someone who could interpret for us. We came to realize that the things of the heart and the things of God are the same in any language."

What has happened since? The story has no end for it continues. Bible schools and evangelistic programs go on; Scripture portions are distributed; and physical care given. The most important thing? "Jesus loves me, this I know, for the Bible tells me so," and so do the people of the Baptist church at Beaufort, South Carolina! An elderly Haitian man said, "God is pleased with what your church is doing, mademoiselle." First John 3:17-18 reads, "But whoso hath this world's good, and seeth his brother have need, and shutteth up his bowels of compassion from him, how dwelleth the love of God in him? My little children, let us not love in word, neither in tongue; but in deed and truth."

Migrants who are poor, uneducated, poorly clothed, unkempt, and often ill give Baptist women an unprecedented opportunity to minister to the spiritual and physical. While not every community will have these seasonal workers, many do and can make this a viable part of their total mission action. To say, "We don't know him" is a cop-out! The Home Mission Board has a splendid guide for working with migrants entitled *Migrants*. State convention offices

(including Woman's Missionary Union); Woman's Missionary Union, SBC; the Brotherhood Commission; and the
Home Mission Board all offer leadership training to give
persons with a willing heart the skills they need to minister
and to witness. The Ministry/Witness Resource Guide, *Migrants,* asks the would-be helper three questions: (1) Do
I really want to help? Do I really want to put myself truly
at the service of another? (2) Am I strong enough to help?
It takes strength to face reality, to risk danger, to allow
those you help to make mistakes, to endure their doubts
and despair. (3) Am I _____ enough to help? The
helper must be able to say, "There, but for the grace of
God, go I."

Approximately 75 percent of the nation's produce will
be harvested this year by more than 2 million migrants as
they move across the United States. They will be blacks
who are concentrated primarily in the eastern part of the
United States, Haitians, Hispanics, and Anglos (non-Latin
whites). You may not see them in fruit orchards, or vege-
table farms, in packing houses and canneries. But if these
places of occupation are in your community, you will see
them in grocery stores, laundromats, on city and village
streets. They are waiting for someone who cares! I hope
you do.

This Is the Big Question

If migrants come regularly to you area will you organize
a "think tank" to determine how their needs might be met
by a mission action group in your church?

6
I Can Minister and Witness to the Homeless

Gladys Steele is a plump red-haired widow whose life was dramatically changed five years ago when she came to know Jesus Christ as Saviour at the Victory Baptist Church in Buena Vista, Virginia. Since then she has made it a habit to look after old, sick people or others who are down on their luck. For years, when a homeless man needed a meal or shelter from the cold, he was likely to wind up on the porch of Gladys Steele's house.

She would give him a plate of beans, a cup of coffee, and some attention to his troubles. From her meager income from veteran's benefits and by collecting castoffs from local stores and friends, she tried to fill needs as she saw them. Gladys knew the homeless for they had once been her drinking buddies. One day five years ago she decided to quit drinking. "I woke up one morning and said, 'This is not the life for me.' "

During the very cold winter of 1986, citizens of the mountain city of Lexington (very near Buena Vista) began looking for a place for a shelter for the homeless. A church offered space, but only when the temperature dropped below 20 degrees. There were hang-ups with other places. Meanwhile, the nights kept getting colder.

Gladys Steele solved the problem. The shelter would be at her house! As soon as that word was out, help began pouring in. A building contractor and electrician made extensive repairs and improvements at cost. Lawyers volunteered their legal services. People brought cots, blankets, and food. Churches gave money; young people painted.

Members of Phi Alpha Delta, a service fraternity at Washington and Lee University School of Law, followed the leadership of Andrew McThenia, a law professor who had spearheaded the organization of the shelter. St. Patrick's Catholic Church moved its meals for the homeless to the shelter.

Local police know Gladys Steele as a one-woman social service agency. "She's a grand lady," they say.

Gladys only says, "I feel that God showed me that this is the way I am needed."

I heard about Gladys when 24 inches of snow were on the ground in our area and it was extremely cold. My husband was out of town and I had been wondering what I would do if someone should knock on my door at night and ask for shelter. The risks were so great! I simply prayed long and seriously that if the need arose, our loving Father would give me the courage to take them in.

The homeless are not always those who need winter shelter. They are children who need temporary shelter from bad home situations, abused wives and husbands, drug abusers, and estranged children.

Rachel Howard is one of these risk takers. She and her husband were rearing three sons in an Atlanta suburb when young people of the 1970s began to become involved in drugs. Rachel saw the need for Christian people to become involved in rescuing bright youngsters who had succumbed to peer pressure. Debbie was one person Rachel took into her home. The Howards gave her food, shelter, and genuine Christian love. There were rules and discipline; there were laughter and tears. Debbie would run away and the Howards would take her back "just one more time." Each time it was with the risk of "what could happen."

26

After high school graduation Debbie attended college and later married.

The risk Rachel took saved a life!

This Is the Big Question

Former President Jimmy Carter has been very active in Habitat for Humanity, building homes for people who might not otherwise ever have adequate housing. Could a mission action group be formed in your church which, with the aid of youth, retired, people, vacationers, and others, would take on a project for upgrading a house in your community? This would provide housing on a temporary basis through a selected agency.

7
I Can Help Prevent and Correct

Christians in America today strongly differ among themselves on ethical issues such as poverty (and its related problems of illiteracy, disease, crime, inadequate housing, and poor education), political justice and human rights, sexual morality, and alcohol and drug abuse. These issues set a wide agenda for responsible Christians and cannot be ignored if we are to love all people and do good to them.

Many of these issues have been addressed by the church in a surface way; the church has not had a real voice. Involvement of individuals gives credibility to what the church says it stands for—sharing the reconciling love of God. Our personal lives must faithfully represent the character of God who has revealed Himself in Jesus Christ. In essence, we must become involved in our world.

Jesus did not say, "At Thanksgiving and Christmas I was hungry and you gave me meat." He did not say, "I was abused and you ignored the risks which were involved and did not take the time to help Me." He did not ignore the aged, unwed mothers, or the poor. He did say, "Inasmuch as ye did it not to one of the least of these, ye did it not to me (Matt. 25:45)."

There are two distinct ways by which we become involved in mission action. As we seriously endeavor to

28

make a positive Christian impact on a hurting world, we may be "preventers" or "correctors." The preventers influence segments of society to keep wrongs from happening. The correctors take people and issues as they exist and seek to bring about healing and reconciliation. Some persons will be both. The stewardship of our Christian influence is called forth to meet the challenges of both moral and social concerns in our communities, not in the name of good citizenship, though this may well be, but in the name of Jesus Christ. The task is too overwhelming to undertake without radical dependence on the Holy Spirit.

As the correctors find the victims of social and moral ills, the preventers discover how to keep others from becoming victims. Finding, correcting, and preventing child abuse is one example. Parents Anonymous and MILK (Mothers Inside Loving Kids) work together to correct and prevent child abuse.

No longer can "I just do not know what to do" or "There's nothing in our community we can do" be said with honesty or accuracy. It can mean that we do not know our community.

My community of 50,000 people is semirural. Most residents hold jobs related to the tobacco and textile industries. These and several other smaller, but less seasonal, industries make the population more heterogeneous than it was 25 years ago. A more mobile society and an age of expanded personal license have made community cooperation necessary. To bring a vital, personal witness to the people of my area, I need to find a source of opportunity. At the time of this writing, I found that 45 different service groups, not counting US government agencies, public schools, and colleges, were already organized and waiting for help from churches. They work with all ages and social and economic groups.

I can be either a "mover" or a "shaker," a political activist or a homebody ministering one on one. I can be a busy pollyanna or a serious Christian trying with the power of the Holy Spirit to minister in Jesus' name.

One day I learned very vividly that opportunities for mission action can come very unexpectedly. I was in a laundromat and a couple entered with an autistic child. The parents looked tired. The mother explained that her hyperacative four-year-old had just come from the Speech and Hearing Clinic (one of those community agencies). A teacher had been trying to get the child to talk. Throat sounds had been her only means of communication. Taking my ever-present pen and pad from my purse, I motioned for the child to "come see." She did. We soon drew her little hand on that piece of paper and named her thumb Jesus. I began a repetition of phrases all beginning with Jesus—loves little blue-eyed girls; Jesus is my good friend; Jesus wants me to talk; and on we went. We drew faces on those fingers and said, "These are Jesus' friends, too." Her span of attention was short and soon she was running again. This time she was saying, "Je, Je, Je." Her brain had connected. I prayed that it had been done in the Master's name.

This Is the Big Question

Do you see yourself as a preventer or a corrector? Outline a plan of action for whichever you chose.

8
I Can Combat Social and Moral Issues

Someone has said recently that the four major problems confronting the American family all begin with the letter *a*—abortion, abuse, AIDS, and alcohol.

To discuss the morality or immorality of these problems is not the responsibility of the writer at this point. The intent here is to draw word pictures and suggest ways Christian women in mission action can ease the hurt of some of society and strengthen the home. The study in each area is inexhaustive and sheer frustration can result when one tries to cover all areas. A survey of the issues in a local community can lead to a decision as to which issue should be addressed by the group.

The horror stories of child abuse catch our eyes almost daily as we read newspapers and listen to the media. Brutal beatings, burnings, and sexual abuse of helpless children furnish stories that raise our tempers and indignations. When we read that 5,000 children out of the 1,500,000 who are abused each year will die from their injuries, we cannot ignore it. Added to that number are aging parents, wives, and husbands who suffer verbal abuse, loss of freedom, and beatings. Some are without day-by-day necessities. The problem of abuse is monumental.

Wesley Monfalcone in *Coping with Abuse in the Family*

has stated that "Everyone is capable of abuse. We all have the potential for the highest and lowest behavior." Abusers may be Christian or non-Christian; they may even be your neighbor. Someone has pointed out that the abuser may be a professing Christian who focuses on "spare the rod and spoil the child" rather than on the admonition of Colossians 3:21 for parents to provoke not their children to wrath. Or, it may be a husband who demands submission from his wife, yet neglects to love her as Christ loved the church.

Each year 282,000 men are beaten by their wives or girlfriends and one in every two wives is abused by her husband. The growing number of elderly who are abused fall into four categories: financial/material, physical, psychological, and neglect. Active neglect occurs when food, medication, etc., are deliberately withheld. Passive neglect happens when the caregiver is unable because of ignorance or inability to meet the older person's needs.

Like child and spouse abuse, the problem cuts across social, racial, and religious lines. Females are most likely victims, simply because there are more of them. Most victims live with their abusers. Eighty percent and upward of known physical abuse is committed by relatives, usually sons; neglect and psychological abuse seems to be the domain of daughters. Sometimes the child is "repaying" the parents for similar treatment given them as a child.

A recent report from the Washington-based Children's Defense Fund gave some startling statistics on the present status of children living in America today: Of every 100 children born today 20 will be born out of wedlock; 13 will be born to a teenage mother; 15 will be born into a household where no parent is employed.

These facts contribute to the long list of things which cause abuse. There is a history of poor interpersonal relationships in which the abusers have not learned to "blow off steam" in a socially acceptable manner. They do not know what the severe stresses of life are doing to them; hence, do not know where and how to get help in handling these stresses. Or, mental illness or drug/alcohol dependence may be involved.

Whatever the cause, abuse is often hard to detect.

In both elder and spouse abuse, the abused decide they would rather stay in a relationship than leave. Fear of future punishment or abandonment keeps others quiet. Like abused wives, many victims have a bad self-image and feel they deserve poor treatment.

But the most powerful reason for silence of the abused is shame. "How can I tell anyone my son assaulted me? What will people think of our family?"

Children are sometimes easier to spot. Repeated and unusual injuries, poor health (which may be caused from malnutrition), unkempt appearances, and disruptive and withdrawn behavior are clues to mistreatment. Children who come from highly isolated families frequently show signs of behavior patterns which need to be modified or corrected by parents. A child from a setting such as this will be terribly afraid of telling of sexual or physical abuse even when it comes from outside the family. Even an older teenager will not be able to talk about such incidents for fear of rejection from parents of unusual standards.

What can we do to help?

Mabel McClellan (Mrs. Albert) is a 70-ish very active grandmother who is a model volunteer with the abused. Through her church, Immanuel Baptist Church of Nashville, Tennessee, she has worked in setting up a church-wide mission action program which is sponsored jointly by the missions and ministry committee of the church and Baptist Women. Mission action volunteers may work jointly, in teams, as individuals, or in community relationships. Primarily, they direct their efforts through four major agencies in Nashville:

St. Patrick's Shelter—a temporary shelter for homeless families and women. Here Baptist Women may spend the night as a part of a team, cook a dish for supper, or serve a meal.

Parents Anonymous Family Abuse Program—a telephone helpline service set up to intervene and modify abusive behavior of parents through telephone conversations. A volunteer mans the helpline on specific days.

YWCA Domestic Violence Shelter—a service providing

temporary shelter, employment counseling, parenting skills, and group support for victims of domestic violence. Here the use of the volunteer, either professionally skilled or unskilled, is limitless. Telephone counselors, seamstresses, cooks, worship leaders, participants, and donors are equally welcomed.

Maternal and Infant Care Program—a program providing a pregnancy test, prenatal and follow-up care for mothers and babies, and a wide range of services for women meeting certain income requirements. Also, classes in parenting, nutrition, and family planning are taught by volunteers. A good photographer is used to make slides for presentation to interested groups.

My town or village is much too small for these, you may say.

Look again at four areas in which Immanual Baptist Church women work through agencies. These same ministries could be done by individuals to individuals.

In addition, all of us can give friendship and encouragement and provide sources of help to those persons who could easily become abusers. This means making some of our time available to them.

Ginny Hendricks, a strong advocate against child abuse, has emphatically said: "You have a moral, and in some cases, a legal responsibility to report child abuse. By law, you cannot be prosecuted for doing so in good faith."

Risa Breckman, Elder Abuse Project director for the Bronx says, "We have to become advocates—for our loved ones, friends, neighbors, clients, and patients. Basically, we have to get involved."

This Is the Big Question

Would you report any evidence of physical abuse, no matter who the victim, to authorities and then pray for wisdom as to how *you* could help the victim?

In 1982 Mary Dan Kuhnle invited my husband and me to lunch at the Sellers Baptist Home and Adoption Center. Present that Saturday for lunch were five girls who had delivered their babies on the previous Thursday. And beside each of their chairs were five bassinet carriers with five beautiful babies. Oh the emotions they brought to the heart!

Here were five girls who had the option between abortion and having their babies. They had chosen life instead of death. In the next month they would choose between adoption and rearing the child as a single parent. In that month each girl would live in a house next door and be in complete charge of herself and the baby. She would cook, wash, clean, stay up nights with a colicky baby, and think of how she would support the child if she chose to keep it. She would receive personal counseling. Above all, she would be shown God's forgiving love.

Sellers Home and Adoption Center is affiliated with the Home Mission Board. Other Christian crisis pregnancy centers have been established and are being run by local churches or groups of churches working cooperatively. In 1986 the Baptist General Convention of Oklahoma became the first state convention to establish crisis pregnancy centers.

In June 1985 the Gail House Maternity Center in Baton Rouge, Louisiana, opened its doors to pregnant, unwed women. The center was the fulfillment of a dream of a childless woman.

Gail Gully Poirer was in the process of adopting a child when cancer was discovered. The Poirers dropped their adoption plans and Gail began working on another plan. With her pastor, Bob Anderson of Parkview Baptist Church in Baton Rouge, she began planning a program which would assist young women who were having to choose between abortion and adoption.

It was a center to keep women in a homelike atmosphere with housing, counseling, prenatal and childbirth education, high school classes, and other activities. The center would also serve as an adoption center for Christian families wanting babies. One woman's dream became the answer to countless other hopes and dreams. Gail died a year before seeing her dream come to reality.

One Baptist Young Women's organization chose to befriend girls in such a center. They took the girls shopping and out to lunch and bought maternity and baby clothes. They did things which build self-esteem. They helped each girl know the job opportunities for which she could be preparing.

While the larger number of unwanted pregnancies occur among teenaged girls, these women are of all ages and come from all socioeconomic walks of life.

The Christian Life Commission has published excellent helps to deal with both preventive education and alternatives to abortion. Women can become strong advocates of the use of these materials by the church. The materials speak loud and clear about the issue, what the church can do, and what individuals can do. The Southern Baptist Convention has set aside a Sanctity of Human Life Sunday and the Christian Life Commission has excellent detailed materials on the subject of the sanctity of human life. Baptist women can encourage the use of them.

The Bible teaches that sex is God's good gift which he intends for the perpetuation, enrichment, and fulfillment of human life. The "one flesh" union referred to in Genesis 2:24 and Matthew 19:5-6 is to be expressed solely within the loving covenant of marriage. Baptist women are not powerless. With their strong commitment to the family and an authentic respect for the sanctity of human life, they can bring the church to understand that abortion is more than a legal problem. Legal prohibitions alone can never solve the problem. Christians must speak out against abuse of sex and sexual promiscuity. Attitudes of Victorian-age silence must be overcome. The apathy of the twentieth-century Christian church in dealing with social issues must be realized as a deterrent to strong human values and family life. Southern Baptists do not agree on all circumstances under which abortion should be available. They do agree that is is not an acceptable means of birth control and that each person involved in the decision related to abortion is responsible and answerable to God— the female, the male, and attending physician.

This Is the Big Question

Teenage pregnancies are at an all-time high in your area. What would you do?

- Say, "If these kids had been brought up properly this would not have happened"?
- Tell your own children to have nothing to do with the pregnant girls?
- Pray for the teenager and her family?
- Become an advocate of sex education in the home and school?
- Organize information in your community giving alternatives to abortion?

Recently I sat in a dental chair for my annual teeth cleaning. The hygienist was wearing a mask and rubber gloves which she had not worn on my previous visits. For the very first time I was faced with the reality of transmission of AIDS.

For months I had been bombarded by the media with statistics and information about the worst medical problem of the twentieth century—Acquired Immune Deficiency Syndrome. The day before my visit to the dentist, the President of the United States had suggested that possible testing for the deadly AIDS virus should be done in the general population.

Leaving the office that day, I thought, What would I do if someone in my family or one of my friends told me he or she had been diagnosed with AIDS? I also wondered, What can we do to get the church ready to respond when the actual need arises?

No longer could we say this was a disease only of homosexuals. No longer could we resist action by being disgusted, angry, indifferent, or fearful. The time has come to bring the problem out in the open.

Presnall Wood, editor of *Texas Baptist Standard,* suggested in his April 29, 1987, editorial three things which must not be condoned: (1) The sin of homosexuality. He gave as Scripture references Leviticus 18:22, 20:3; Romans 1:26-27; and 1 Corinthians 6:9-10 which present homosexuality as sin. (2) Sexual promiscuity. Monogamous sex within marriage is mandated by God. Extramarital sex is wrong. (3) Hate toward the victims of AIDS. Though large numbers (90 percent or above) of persons got the virus from promiscuous sexual activity and sharing of needles by drug users, innocent people, including children, have become victims. The mother of a four-year-old who got AIDS through a blood transfusion said, "You need to remember that these AIDS victims are sick and dying; forget the moral judgement and stigma; they still need spiritual counseling."

The surgeon general of the United States, C. Everett Koop, has stated that by the end of 1990, 250,000 people will have contracted Acquired Immune Deficiency Syndrome. This, he said, is much like the situation in Europe several centuries ago when smallpox and bubonic plague destroyed hundreds of thousands of lives and changed the course of history.

In a report compiled at the directive of the President of the United States, Koop said to the President and cabinet on October 27, 1986:

"Education concerning AIDS must start at the lowest grade possible as part of any health and hygiene program. There is no doubt that we need sex education in schools and it must include information on heterosexual and homosexual relationships. The threat of AIDS should be sufficient to permit a sex education curriculum with a heavy emphasis on prevention of AIDS and other sexually transmitted diseases.

"It remains my wish that parents will be primary teachers of sex and human relations to children. The task should not be left by default to movies, television, or the street corner."

To the church he said, "America's children don't live in a vacuum; therefore, we must all work together to help our children grow up and cope with the real world of pleasure and danger. That's the reason why our schools, churches, synagogues, and other community institutions must provide our children with the best possible information—physical, sexual, emotional, and psychological—

to help them negotiate their own way through the human condition."

The serious question for mission action is, What can be done in response to this horrible problem? Again Jesus' teaching in Matthew 25 must be our guideline: "Whenever you refused to help one of the least of these important ones, you refused to help me" (Matt. 25:45 TEV).

Wood also directed some comments to the church. He said, "The church, as well as society, could be tested by AIDS. There must be some stable, Bible-based Christian thinking and leadership to prevent panic in the church because of the panic of AIDS."

Christians need to teach children the following three things: (1) Part of the cure for AIDS has already been found in living according to God's plan. (2) Abstain from sex until you are married. (3) Extramarital sex is wrong. Maintain a faithful monogamous relationship with one faithful partner after marriage.

In every church a missions organization or a concerned individual could offer some help. They might (1) get all available accurate information on the transmission of the disease and see that people are properly informed; (2) consult with local doctors regarding safe but supportive ways the missions organization could relate to the victims of AIDS (i.e., letters, Scripture portions, offer of specific prayer support); (3) go immediately to the families of the patient to share God's love and offer help by being "listeners," preparing family meals, caring for small children or elderly in the home, chauffeuring, etc; (4) ask for a task force from the church to work with the mission action group to draw up guidelines for ministry by the church.

This Is the Big Question

Would you be willing to be a spokesperson for proper AIDS education in your community?

STOPP, SMART, MADD, PRIDE, AA, REACH

A list of new detergents? Names for pain-relieving drugs for arthritis? Emphatically, no!

These are organizations working beside nearly 40 similar ones to combat the most sinister problem facing families today—alcohol.

Alcohol has become a deadly problem because it is hidden, socially acceptable as a drug, and easily available. It is the crutch most likely grabbed in time of stress and peer pressure.

A survey done in 1983 by *Weekly Reader* showed that almost one-half of children aged 9-12 reported peer pressure to drink. In two short years PRIDE (Parent Resource Institute for Drug Education) reported that 43 percent of 6,155 seventh-graders were experimenting with hard liquor. Further statistics show that nearly 10,000 young people die each year in accidents directly related to imbibing.

What starts these youngsters to thinking about "trying just one"? (1) They see relatives and family friends drinking. (2) They "want to belong." (3) Somebody has told them that drinking is more desirable than smoking marijuana or snorting cocaine. What was clearly an adult problem 25 years ago, has become a problem that knows no age. A 17-year-old told of his first drink at age five when he sneaked champagne at a family New Year's Eve party. This began a stint of secret drinking which did not become known until he was 10. While serving as an altar boy, he drank several bottles of sacramental wine and threw up during the communion service.

In 1984, the Southern Baptist Convention passed a resolution that called for a ban on alcohol ads in the broadcast media. Christian Life Commission staff member Harry Hollis joined thousands of supporters of a project called SMART (Stop Marketing Alcohol on Radio and Television) which called for an end to alcohol ads or equal time for health messages about alcohol. Hollis took the Southern Baptist Convention resolution with him to the Senate subcommittee on alcoholism and drug abuse. To date only hard liquor ads have been removed. Beer and wine ads continue to entice.

Mothers Against Drunk Driving (MADD) have lobbied to see that stiffer penalties were given drunken drivers. This one organization alone has shown what women who band together can do.

In hundreds of high schools across the country, young people are organizing STOPP (Students to Offset Peer Pressure) groups. These groups provide non-drug and alcohol activities to show that it is popular to say no to drugs and still have good fun. The Just Say No to Drugs program had more than 5,000,000 youngsters in Walk Against Drugs in 1986.

All of these and others are drops in the mighty ocean of substance abuse. They are beginning efforts to halt the number one drug problem—alcohol.

Joining any or all of these national groups does not constitute mission action. They serve as excellent resources for missions organizations and to motivate missions organizations to deal with substance abuse on a local level. While the purpose of these secular organizations is excellent, mission action serves the added dimension of specifically healing the soul as the body is healed.

Woman's Missionary Union of First Baptist Church in Laurel, Mississippi, sponsored a churchwide mission action project on alcohol and other drug abuse. A two-part educational television special "The Chemical People" was shown on consecutive Sunday evenings. Parents continued to meet on Wednesday evenings for several weeks to share information and educate themselves concerning alcohol use. Church members were encouraged to write or call legislators in support of legislation against alcohol.

These educational opportunities gave church families the facts, the motivation, and the suggestions as to how they could deal with the alcohol/drug abuse situations in their community. Two very important results were (1) parents were taught to recognize both alcohol and drug effects and dependencies; (2) they affirmed each other as a group to forthrightly deal with community problems.

Missions organizations consist of loving, caring persons who want the best results so that families may live together bound by the Spirit of Christ rather than spirits of the devil. Groups which choose to reach beyond the church to those caught in the throes of alcohol abuse have many avenues of service. They can (1) train themselves to recognize drinkers; (2) encourage drinkers to join supportive groups such as Alcoholics Anonymous if the problem is severe; (3) build esteem and self-confidence where persons are drinking to belong; (4) become political activists to work for tougher laws on drunk driving; and (5) do what a high school senior said was the best way to fight drug abuse—educate, educate, educate.

And to educate means beginning in the church with what the Bible has to say about alcohol. The Christian Life Commission has material and a videotape available at small cost. They can be a starting point to education on a family destroyer.

This Is the Big Question

Would you help establish a telephone hotline for alcoholics who are trying not to drink and want somebody to talk with them?

Postlude

These issues are only a part of the array of problems facing women who do mission action. As society changes, Baptist women must be aware of new issues which take their places beside already-existing problems.

Social changes in this age are coming about so rapidly we are faced with new problems every day. My sincere belief is that the church must come with the prophetic voice for the twenty-first century that it did when it emerged from the Dark Ages and brought about the Protestant Reformation. While *abortion* has been the catchword of the past ten years, the church has yet to speak in clear tones regarding test-tube babies, in vitro fertilization, surrogate mothers, and the list goes on. God does not instruct us at any point to be judges; He does call us to be His witnesses and show His love.

"You are my friends if you do what I command you. ... This, then, is what I command you: love one another" (John 15:14, 17 TEV).

42

Are You Ready for Personal Witnessing—A Checkup

1. Do you really want to make the good news relevant to people outside your church?
2. How do you talk about Jesus Christ to
   a) an office worker who has just been replaced by a computer?
   b) the victim of a divorce who was also the victim of a broken home and who doesn't trust anybody?
   c) a highly trained scientist who thinks that "life" in a test tube is imminent?
   d) the lonely "has everything" woman in your neighborhood who pretends that her lack of interaction with people is due to their inferiority?
3. Do you believe that obedience in evangelism is one of the keys to spiritual health?
4. Jesus witnessed to the woman at the well near Sychar by going beyond His social circle. Are you afraid to get to know non-Christians?
5. Some believe that witnessing is being able to quote a lot of Scripture verses to a non-Christian. Witnessing involves all that we are and therefore do. It goes far beyond what we say at certain inspired moments. The question is not *Will* we witness (speak)? but *How* will we witness? Will you be Christ's witness?

PART II

I Can Do Personal Witnessing

9
I Can Do What Jesus Commanded

Faces of the children haunt me most: empty eyes, tattered clothes, sheepish grins. They beg for food, plead for money.

A little boy stood at our gate and rang the doorbell. He held a paperbag in one hand and the gate with the other. He pressed his face between the bars and asked for food.

I was certain his sack was full of food, and I wasn't about to be fooled into giving him more. Smugly, I motioned for him to open it.

He ducked his head and timidly opened his sack. It held the only change of clothing he owned. It was then I realized the child has no family—no home—no one to care.

As I filled his bag with fruit and vegetables, I prayed, "Lord, give me the wisdom. Send me strength. Grant that I may be a mirror of your never-ending love. Here am I. Send me. Send me."[1]

According to the New Testament, the good news is first and foremost for the poor and outcast. To read and reread the witness of Jesus is to see Him as a poor man Who identified with the powerless and oppressed and to hear Him say, "I have come that you may have life and have it more abundantly." The privileged place of the poor and outcast in the kingdom was stated so succinctly in Matthew 11:25 (NASB) in Jesus' prayer, "I praise thee, O Father . . . that Thou didst hide these things from the wise and intelligent and didst reveal them to babes." "The babes" were the harassed and helpless multitude to whom Jesus sent His disciples to heal and to announce the kingdom (Matt. 10:1,7), and the heavy laden and weary whom Jesus personally invited unto himself (Matt. 11:28).

John's and Luke's Gospels paint the special role of outsiders in the kingdom as Jesus ministers to Samaritans who revealed a greater sensitivity to the presence of the kingdom than many Jews. In Acts, Luke tells the story of the poverty program of the earliest church—a community which took care of widows, made room for Samaritans and Gentiles, was able to transcend the barriers of class and race, and was taken care of in poverty and want by its Gentile daughter churches.

To witness personally to persons in their lostness wherever they are—ghetto, city street, neighborhood, ranch, or plantation—is to tell them that Jesus Christ can radically change the frail, the unjust, and death-prone pattern of human existence. God sent Jesus to bring into being a new world order. That wonderfully exciting news was actually born in the first four words of the Bible, "In the beginning God," and in the sheer power of His word, "And God said. . . ."

Jesus in the very first beatitude sets forth His teaching on the "blessedness" of being "poor in spirit." Rarely, very rarely, does one consider it a blessing to be poor in anything!

William Barclay in his commentary on Matthew helps us understand the word *poor* through his explanation of two Greek words meaning poor: *penēs* which describes the man who has nothing superfluous, and *ptōchos* which describes the man who has nothing at all. Jesus used the latter. Then Barclay further explains the Aramaic which Jesus would have been speaking: *'ani* and *ebiōn* describe the poor, humble, helpless man who puts his whole trust in God. Putting the two definitions together Barclay writes: "Blessed is the man who has realised his own utter helplessness, and who puts his whole trust in God" (*The Gospel of Matthew,* p. 91).

We will become detached from things when we know they do not have it in them to bring happiness and security.

48

We will become completely attached to God Who can bring hope, help, and strength.

Jesus never called actual material poverty a good thing. His teaching in Matthew 25 clearly points out that He does give material things to some and expects them in return to take care of those who are in need. Matthew 25:35-40 has long been the guidepost for mission action but it must be remembered that the parable of the talent immediately precedes it. As individuals, as churches, and as a denomination, we have an awesome responsibility for we have much. We say as the rich young ruler, "Ever since I was young, I have obeyed all these commandments." But Jesus shakes his head sadly and repeats, "Sell all you have and give the money to the poor . . . and come follow me" (Luke 18:22 TEV).

Jesus also used many opportunities with the not-so-poor as witness to Who He was—the wedding at Cana, dinner at Pharisee Simon's home, healing the Roman official's daughter, the visit with Mary and Martha. Perhaps one of the most unnoticed connections in the New Testament is in John 3. It was to the important and affluent Nicodemus the Pharisee that Jesus spoke the most important words of the Bible, "For God loved the world so much that he gave his only son, so that everyone who believes in him may not die but have eternal life" (John 3:16 TEV).

"O the bliss of the man who has realized his own utter helplessness and who has put his whole trust in God. For thus alone he can render to God that perfect obedience which will make him a citizen of the kingdom of Heaven."

Annemarie Schuh left her Bavarian home in 1978 to study at the University of Berlin. In 1983, she enrolled in the University of Missouri's prestigious school of journalism. Her story could have ended with her becoming a world renowned journalist in Europe. It does not, as such.

During her first month in the United States, Annemarie attended a Baptist church "just out of curiosity." It was a witnessing church and through the witness of that congregation she was led to accept Christ and later to be baptized. She had never been inside a German Baptist church. It was not until this young woman had been called of God to vocational ministry and met some representatives of the German Baptist Union who came to Southern Baptist Theological Seminary in Louisville, Kentucky, that she heard someone pray in her own language.

After seminary training at Southern and at Ruschlikon Baptist Theological Seminary in Switzerland and post-doctoral work in a European university, Annemarie wants to continue to work in personal evangelism and teach religion or theology in a European university. When someone asked her what her goal in life was, her quick reply was, "To be a visible vessel for God's working power."

What if no one had ever told her of that power? How do we who are Christ's followers hear the call to be the church in the latter part of the twentieth century? With apathy? With frustrated concern? With a determination to get a handle on how to be the champions of the poor? With a boldness to consistently witness to those in the upper economic level?

When we analyze each day's events we must be aware of the countless times we had the opportunity to witness both by our actions and words to the joy of a Christ-controlled life. Many times our best witness is how stressful times are handled and how we listen to the non-Christian's words. Jesus was the quiet listener for the woman at the well in Samaria. Then, at the appropriate time, He gave her the good news.

Let us give more to helping the poor for, "Whoever knows what is right to do and fails to do it, for him it is sin" (James 4:17 KJV).

This Is the Big Question

Have you ever really considered that you are Jesus Christ to a lot of people? Tremendous responsibility and privilege are entrusted to us as representatives of Christ. Write the names of two persons—one poor and one affluent—to whom you are to witness. Read 1 Peter 2:21.

---

[1]"To Be a Mirror." Letter from Laurie Taylor (missionary in Brazil) in "Epistle," *The Commission*, September 1986, 72.

10
I Can Tell What I Have Seen

Perhaps the application of the Scriptures to our daily lives has become more and more difficult as "we are carried by the waves and blown about by every shifting wind." We, with the disciples of Christ, find the teachings of Jesus hard. Jesus, personally, and very humanly, showed that following God's will is not easy.

Jesus did not give up when the Jews rejected His efforts to point them to a vital, living faith. He continued shaping His people. He chose 12 students (disciples) to become authorized spokesmen (apostles) and commissioned them to serve.

Then Jesus gave His disciples guidance on how to live. In Luke 7 we read His sermon on the plains. In this account Jesus shows His disciples that it is faith in God which transforms talk about God to obedience to Him. John the Baptist was no doubt wondering why Jesus did not become the Messiah and free him from his imprisonment at the fortress Machaerus. So, John sent his disciples to ask Jesus if He was really the expected Messiah. (That question has not faded from our minds in times of anxiety even today as we cry out, "Lord, if you are really who you say you are. . . .")

Jesus simply said, "Go back and tell John what you have seen and heard. . . . How happy are those who have no doubts about me." He did not demean John the Baptist. He just showed John the new standards of the kingdom. Jesus called attention once again to self-giving love.

The Pharisees did not accept this; they much preferred living by a set of rules rather than opening themselves to a new way of life. Twentieth-century life is not much different. Yet in the restlessness of our souls there is a yearning to be different than we are, to break out of the cold, listless molds of our lesser selves and be who we might yet become.

Ours is classified as an age of technology. In the past 60 years more scientific discoveries have been made than in all other years of civilization put together, but we live in confusion. Technology has not made us happy; poverty still exists. Peace is as elusive as ever; and men who once exercised a deep personal faith in God no longer do so. Modern human beings, their loss of confidence notwithstanding, are still seeking for that to which they may wholeheartedly commit their lives.

In reflection on the literacy program of Each One Teach One, Dr. Frank Laubach, the founder, said that all who had worked on the literacy program felt they were involved in a purpose they only dimly understood. They later realized that God was using them to help people read His word. He also said that they alone could not have laid a foundation for the literacy program without Him.

The truth is that the chief sources of dignity and equality for all people are found in biblical heritage.

Living in the "after" side of the Resurrection, the joyous, bursting enthusiasm of the women running from the tomb to give the disciples the message of the angel was interrupted when they saw Jesus running ahead of them. He was alive and to be experienced in a new way.

When we accept the kind of life the Resurrection was intended to bring, we want to give the world the Easter news that God was in Christ reconciling the world unto Himself. Winfred Moore at First Baptist Church, Amarillo, Texas, said in his Easter 1986 church bulletin, "No longer be satisfied with growing morning glorys when you could grow roses."

52

David Watson, a canon in the Anglican church and a worldwide leader in evangelism and renewal, has said that the great majority of Western Christians (church members, Bible readers, even born-again Christians) are not true disciples of Jesus; and if they were, there would be a staggering impact on society.

Jesus started small—12 men who were very different, ordinary, and unlettered. On them, with the close tutoring of Jesus, would depend the entire future of the Christian church. One would fail completely and the others would disappoint the Master. But Jesus persisted with them, loving them to the end and laying a firm foundation for the whole church of God.

In the old Testament we also read of God calling out and preparing people to serve Him. Elisha's farm lay in the lowliest part of Palestine, in the fertile, abundantly watered valley south of the Sea of Galilee. Here in this secure and pleasant setting, Elisha had expected to live out his days.

Suddenly in the very act of turning a furrow, a mantle was placed on his shoulders. Turning to see the aging prophet Elijah, Elisha at once understood and was terrified. That gesture meant "You are to succeed me, Elisha!" Someday this farmer would wear the cloak of the famous prophet Elijah. A calling could scarcely be more daunting.

Then it was as if suddenly Elijah seemed appalled at the sacrifice he proposed. "Go back," he cried, "for what have I done to you!" Elisha needed no more time. He dropped the plow without finishing the field.

Elijah meanwhile had not broken his stride. The old prophet was on his way and the younger man ran after him with a resounding "Yes!"

It was general knowledge that Elijah's ministry was nearing its end. A group of 50 men from Jericho followed the two companions that final day as far as the banks of the Jordan River. There Elijah rolled up his old goatskin mantle—the one he had symbolically thrown across Elisha's shoulders—and struck the surface of the stream. Awed, the 50 witnesses watched the waters part and the two companions crossed over.

Out of sight of the curious crowd, Elijah turned for the last time to his faithful follower, Elisha.

"Ask what I can do for you," he invited, "before I am taken from you."

Elisha answered without hesitation, "Let me inherit a double share of your spirit." He had asked for a spiritual inheritance—in an abundance that would let him continue his master's ministry.

Down the centuries the Son of God is willing to prepare others to continue His ministry.

Make me a mirror of God's continuous shaping. And, Lord, give me a double share of Your love.

This Is the Big Question

A witness must be accurate or he is charged with perjury. Write three things you know that Jesus Christ has done in your life.

11
I Can Be a Witnessing Servant

Which one of us does not respond to the thrilling music, both choral and instrumental, of Handel's *Messiah*? Coupled with the always fresh story of the Christ child, minds and hearts respond to the Prince of Peace, the Everlasting Father. When Christmas is over, how many wish to walk with the Suffering Servant?

Only by being the Servant-Messiah could Jesus provide redemption for His people and leave them a clear path to follow in His steps. He was the Servant of the Lord and His primary mission was to call others to serve God.

Delos Miles, professor of Evangelism at Southeastern Baptist Theological Seminary, delivered the charge to the graduates of the June 1986 class. He noted that hero worship would impede the progress of a spiritual journey. Miles warned, "Don't look to a great cloud of witnesses for your model. Jesus offers you the servant model and all others are marred and scarred by sin."

Urging the graduates to exhibit a loving, suffering servant leadership style, he said, "The greatest compliment you can receive is to be told, 'you remind me of Jesus Christ.'"

Like the Jews of Jesus' day, we see ourselves as the Lord's suffering servants, but in what we do for others rather than in obedience to the lordship of Christ. Martha misunderstood the servant role when she chose to be the cook. We choose the busy things of ministry before we make complete allegiance to the Father. Busy-ness is not witnessing!

Jesus was baptized; He prayed; the heavens opened and the Holy Spirit descended upon Him. Then He received the commendation, "You are my own dear Son. I am pleased with You." Our servanthood to God begins with our willingness to obey and the receiving of the Holy Spirit. Power now received, we are ready in self-giving love for a life of service to those without Christ.

All our skills and tools of personal witnessing fail if there is not the connection of the Holy Spirit. Perhaps we can see the importance of connection with an illustration from a sports event.

In the fall of 1986, a University of Miami football player, Vinny Testaverde, was the most highly acclaimed player in college rankings. At the end of the season, Miami and Penn State were paired in the Fiesta Bowl in Tempe, Arizona, to determine the number one team in college football. Both teams were undefeated. Testaverde had led Miami to defeat Oklahoma, top college team in the 1985 season, in the first game of the 1986 season. Every condition was right for another win, but Miami lost; the players could not connect with the passes.

That is the essential. What persons do for the cause of Christ in the world must be through connection which is the leadership of the Holy Spirit.

If we set before ourselves the task of bringing the world to Christ, we have all the unbelief, inertia, and hostility of the world to resist us. If we do as we are bidden in Acts 1:8 (TEV), "But when the Holy Spirit comes upon you, you will be filled with power, and you will be witnesses for me in Jerusalem, in all of Judea and Samaria, and to the ends of the earth," we have all of the impulse and might of His own life and love to carry us forward in our work. An unknown sage has pointed out that the order is not "Ye shall be witnesses unto me," but, "you shall be my witnesses." We sing "Christ for the World," not "The World for Christ." The object of our mission is that every person

56

shall have an opportunity to hear and respond to the good news that God in Christ is reconciling the world unto Himself.

Being filled with the Holy Spirit, our weary, mundane-filled bodies obey His summons. We refresh our souls with the vision of that time when "they shall not teach every man his neighbor and every man his brother, saying 'Know ye the Lord'; for all shall know Him, from the least unto the greatest."

Let us not dwell on the lord of visions. Let us see before us family, friends, neighbors, and community who are without Christ and use the power of the Holy Spirit to witness.

Not only does the Holy Spirit empower us, but He gives us gifts to boost our confidence. Ralph Neighbour in *This Gift Is Mine* says, "It is the privilege of God to bestow His gifts upon His children. He decides, without any advice from the children, *what* gifts shall be given to each of them" (p. 33). Isn't that just like God? We do not even have to ask! If we did, we would constantly be discarding and asking for something else. These are grace gifts, neither deserved nor earned. We are given that which God knows suits us. By combining the lists from Romans 12:6-13, 1 Corinthians 12:8-10 and 28-30, along with Ephesians 4:11 and 1 Peter 4:10-11, one could find 23 different gifts listed.

Belhaven is a small town in coastal North Carolina. Because of its location, very near productive waters, *fishing* is a well-understood word. The Baptist church of Belhaven wanted to become a church whose members also "fished" for people. In a missions/witnessing weekend seminar, they began studying the gift passages. Every single person was convinced that he or she possessed at least one of the mentioned gifts.

Then the measuring was turned to finding the total number of gifts in the membership. How many of the 23 were possessed by members? They discovered that all 23 gifts listed in the four passages were possessed by someone in that church. What a church!

Then they turned to persons who needed a witness in that community. Matching gifts with personal needs, they blitzed the area on a Saturday night, witnessing to people who needed to know what Jesus Christ could do in a life.

In many communities the horror stories of daily events are heard, read, and bemoaned; but very few Christians turn off the television, put down the newspaper, and go out to "position" themselves for Jesus. Do you?

A comparative study of witnesses and nonwitnesses in the Southern Baptist Convention revealed that the three top hindrances to witnessing were (1) lack of dependence on the Holy Spirit; (2) lack of knowledge about witnessing; and (3) personality is not the type to do personal witnessing. Interestingly, both witnesses and nonwitnesses gave the same hindrances but in a different order.

Elton Trueblood, in *The Incendiary Fellowship*, said that the Christian should be actively involved in the world to prevent its decaying—just as salt is used to preserve meat. Jesus said, "I came to cast fire upon the earth and I wish it were already kindled." Trueblood also said that we need to remember that Jesus did not come to suggest mild religious methods, but "to cast fire on the earth." And that no matter how inadequate we are as kindling, we are called to be elements of that fire.

Witnessing occurs when people are so enkindled by contact with the central fire of Christ that they, in turn, set others on fire. Make a chart of your periods of enthusiasm for doing the work of God. List the people who motivate you to want to witness. You may be surprised. It may not be an eloquent, highly articulate speaker, but the sincere testimony of one sharing an experience with Christ.

This is the Big Question

Did you ever consider imposition a part of servanthood (i.e., *having* to bake cookies for Girls in Action to take to the nursing home; *having* to listen to the talkative alcoholic in your neighborhood; *having* to do church visitation on Tuesday night)? Read Romans 3:5-9.

12
I Can Share My Faith

Bonnie Haight is a paraoptometric who confidently believes that the redeemed of the Lord should say so. She says, "Psalm 107:2 doesn't say how to say so. It just says say so!"

Bonnie lives in Ulster, Pennsylvania, and is a member of the Saco Road Baptist Church in Towanda, Pennsylvania. Brought up in Sunday School and church through her teen years and into adulthood, she knew about Jesus. However, it was not until she was a young mother that Bonnie came to know Jesus in a real way.

One afternoon Bonnie put her elbows on the window sill of her bedroom. Looking out into the beautiful countryside she longingly asked God, "Is this all there is?" A fine husband, a beautiful home, and a badly wanted baby boy were not satisfying. Bonnie was seeking. She lacked something, but she did not know what.

An aunt invited Bonnie to her church. That evening a church group from Alabama was presenting a puppet show and preaching. Bonnie had a conflicting meeting on Monday, but on Tuesday she went "to get her off my back and get it over with."

The half-hour puppet show was entertaining. Then the children were taken from the auditorium to another room for crafts and Bible study. Bonnie tells the story of her experience that night.

"A man got behind the pulpit and began to preach. I

59

had never heard anyone preach like that before—he talked about sin, being born again, Jesus, and heaven. It was overwhelming!

"At the close of the sermon he gave an invitation. I had never been in a church like that before. So I just sat. He invited us back saying there would be puppets and preaching all week.

"I had just heard about a Jesus I never knew, and this preacher seemed to know Jesus so well that I just had to go back! By Thursday night I was under such conviction I could hardly stand it. On Friday night when the invitation was given, my knees were shaking but somehow I walked to the front. The pastor asked me if I really wanted to trust Jesus with my life and become a new creature. My life has not been the same since that October night."

Bonnie began sharing this newfound faith immediately. Within a year—and in God's own timing—she led her son, her best friend, her husband, and her father to a new life in Jesus. At the time of this writing Bonnie's real burden is her boss for whom she has worked for more than 20 years. Because Bonnie is so concerned, she has people all over the country praying for this man.

This beautiful red-haired young woman says, "Life has not been all honey and roses since I became a Christian, but I know that nothing is going to happen that God and I can't handle together."

The church in the world today is not rocking the boat because it does not feel the excitement that the early church felt. Christians in the first century were easily identified because they told everybody what Jesus was doing in their lives. When the late Peter Marshall was chaplain of the United States Senate, he was known for the prayers he prayed. I remember him best for saying that when the early Christians preached, there were either riots or regenerations.

That is the mandate!

The Great Commission as given in Matthew 28:18-20 was the King's order for all generations, for all Christians. In the early church no hierarchical relationship existed. Paul made it clear in Galatians 2 that he considered his

60

authority equal to that of James, John, and Peter. All were to realize then, as we do in the twentieth century, that to bring the gospel of Christ to others is both joy and privilege.

Ophelia Humphrey was selected to write *Witnessing Women* because she was the witnessing woman—in her home state of Texas, in her hometown of Amarillo, and around the world in partnership evangelism. After she wrote the guide, hundreds of women were motivated to do what they thought they could not do—witness to others of their faith. When I asked Ophelia to tell me of a recent experience she had in sharing her faith, she exclaimed, "Oh, let me tell you of one even better!"

"Recently," she said, "I was in the grocery store when a woman came up to me and said, "Aren't you the 'witnessing woman'?" Understanding what she meant, I laughed and said, "Well, yes, I guess I am!"

This woman then related how a group had studied *Witnessing Women* and had gone out to bring others to know Jesus.

The secret is Ophelia Humphrey practices what she preaches!

This Is the Big Question

A non-Christian on being asked what she thought after spending a Sunday evening in a young people's meeting and evening church service answered, "There are some people who have it and some people who don't."
What is the faith you have to offer the world?

13
I Can Use Unexpected Opportunities

One of the most intriguing chapter titles I ever saw was "Catching Chariots." Immediately, I recalled the chariots of the movie *Ben Hur* which had captivated me as a child. Of course I read the chapter!

It came from a splendid book on witnessing written by Jerry Vines, co-pastor of the First Baptist Church of Jacksonville, Florida. Vines used this positive idea to point out the unexpected opportunities God gives Christians to speak to persons who are receptive to the gospel of Christ. It recalls the story of Philip and the eunuch.

Philip had just come from a very successful revival in Samaria. The persecution in Jerusalem had caused this Grecian Jew to go into Samaria, not to hide from the Pharisee heresy hunters, but to preach Christ. Nothing—certainly not the creed or roll of souls without the good news—could keep this deacon from declaring the gospel of grace to the hated Samaritans. Soon the Spirit called him on another mission—to declare the gospel to men of different skin coloring.

An angel of the Lord instructed Philip to go south on the road from Jerusalem to Gaza. As he walked along the road, the Holy Spirit led him to "run over" to a chariot he had seen. When he heard what the Ethiopian eunuch rider was reading he was immediately ready to "Catch the Chariot."

It was just the text Philip needed to declare the atonement Jesus had made on the cross. "And Philip opened his mouth and preached unto him Jesus."

There is joy to be experienced far beyond any expectation when a new convert comes into the kingdom. Why, then, are we afraid? Are we concerned with rejection? Afraid of being offensive? Or, just plain afraid of failure?

Jesus must have seen this fear in His own disciples and the 72 apostles He sent out. He must have known that centuries later fear would be the reason the twentieth-century Christians would still be reticent to witness. In Luke 9 and 10, the plan which Jesus had for overcoming fear is presented. He gave specific instructions to the apostles: (1) they were to preach and heal; (2) they were not to be concerned with personal things; (3) they were to have singleness of purpose; (4) they were not to be concerned with the results. And, they were to go with power and authority. Jesus' plan works. Thousands of words have been written, hundreds of plans presented as method. None have ever superceded Jesus' instructions. The thrust of world evangelization thus begun, it has never failed. It always calls forth the same satisfaction as it did with the 72. "The seventy-two men came back with great joy."

David Watson has asked how Western Christians can overcome their natural reserve and let the good news flow from our churches to where the people are.

Several years ago, when my husband and I were visiting in some of the large cities of Australia, we asked about church growth in this large South Pacific country. The answer from our Christian friends was discouraging, "The union is everything! People consider the church irrelevant!"

In a span of less than ten years that fact has dramatically changed. Spiritual renewal began in the churches and this led to "gossiping about the gospel!" Trade unionists, teachers, and politicians became committed Christians and turned the church into the "light of the world" and the "salt of the earth." The world goes bad when, like meat, it doesn't have the salt.

When the body of Christ, the church, finds God, it can no longer argue about Him but, rather, must fall on its knees in worship and then rise to do His bidding in the midst of the suffering world.

David Barrett in *World-Class Cities and World Evangelization* cites Kittel's full definition of evangelize.

"*Evangeizesthai* (*evangelism*) is not just speaking and preaching: it is proclamation with full authority and power. Signs and wonders accompany the evangelical message. They belong together for the word is powerful and effective. *Evangeizesthai* (*evangelism*) is to offer salvation. It is the powerful proclamation of the good news, the impartation of *soteria* (*salvation*)."

Barrett further notes that "The English word *evangelize* was first used in the first English Bible by John Wycliffe in the year 1382. After his death his followers issued a revised Bible changing *evangelize* throughout to *preach*. *Evangelize* does not therefore occur as a word in the English Bible for the next 600 years."

David Watson has noted that while not every Christian is called to be an evangelist, all are called to be witnesses. While some have the spiritual gifts of the evangelist, there are four marks of a witness: (1) A witness must have firsthand experience of Christ. People will listen only to what we have personally seen and heard. (2) A witness must be able to express himself verbally. We must be ready at all times to answer anyone who asks us to explain the hope we have. (3) A witness must have confidence in the power of God. He knows that without God he can do nothing, but that with God all things are possible. (4) A witness must have compassion for the spiritually lost. He must care for them as individuals who matter deeply to God.

There is an interesting note in Luke 9:9. The latter part of the verse reads, "And he [Herod] kept trying to see Jesus." The reputation of Jesus had preceded Him in the villages and towns into which He would go preaching and healing. Herod, the ruler of Galilee, thought he had covered his sins by beheading John the Baptist. John had accused Herod of many sins. Herod became afraid and confused when he heard Jesus preaching like John had. Herod

64

wanted to see who was causing all this talk!

This was only a beginning. As followers of Jesus saw and felt His forgiving power, they began to witness boldly of what He had done in their lives. Words alone would not accomplish what they were experiencing. Unbelievers watched their lives. Once empowered by the spirit, they began to witness by their words and their walk. They did not wait until they could call a pastor, redecorate the church building, take a census, or organize committees. Had they not received power for their world mission beginning right where they were? Were they not of one mind in Christ and toward one another? In the power of the spirit and as one fellowship of Christ, they were ready to "Catch a Chariot."

W. R. Cullom was professor of Bible at Wake Forest College (now University) before his death. He once related the story of conducting prayer meeting one night at Southern Baptist Theological Seminary in Louisville, Kentucky. Walking home that evening, he overheard two young students discussing the service. The young woman said to her young male friend, "That last hymn tonight always brings me a feeling of despondency. I am doing so little good in the world."

The hymn?

There are lowly hearts to cherish,
There are weary souls who perish,
O, the good we all may do
While the days are going by.

Oh God, remove my blindspots and let me recognize the opportunities to catch my chariots as they come my way.

This Is the Big Question

As we move out of the personal safety zone and get involved with the real world the more opportunities God gives us to bear witness of Jesus Christ. Are you learning how to move into the world genuinely loving your fellowman and asking God, "Which one do you want me to care for?"

Study Guide

The purpose of this book study is for participants to examine the call to mission action and personal witnessing and to determine ways they can live out these tasks in the world around them.

The book is designed for either individual or group study. Individual study may be done by reading the book and completing the This Is the Big Question sections in each chapter. Group study plans are given below. Church Study Course credit is available for either method of study.

Preparation

1. Read the book and respond to the This Is the Big Question section in each chapter.
2. Determine the length of the study. Remember, a minimum of 2½ hours of study is necessary to receive Church Study Course credit. Participants must also read the book.
3. Collect resources. You will want to have on hand copies of WMU magazines, plus other materials which provide training helps or are tools for mission action or personal witnessing. Check the WMU Materials Catalog in the current WMU Year Book for resources.
4. Publicize the study through the church bulletin and newsletter, posters in prominent locations, personal contacts, and announcements. Use the phrase *Learn how to be a mirror of God's love. Come to . . .* in all publicity.
5. Read the instructions below for conducting the study. Choose which ones you will do. Make arrangements for assistance if needed and prepare materials for each activity.
6. Purchase several copies of the book to use in the conference. Arrange for copies to be available for conferees to purchase.

During the study

1. Introductory activity: Near the entrance of the room, place a large mirror on a table. Letter these words on the mirror with tempera paint or on a strip of paper taped to the mirror: *I am a mirror of God's love when I. . . .*
2. Place a stack of slips of paper on the table. Provide the following instructions: Complete this statement: *I am a mirror of God's love when I. . . .* When participants have completed the statement, ask them to share their responses with another person.
3. Ask if some will share their responses. After several have done so, say: We are to be a mirror of God's love to persons who do not know Him. In many cases, we need to meet physical or social needs as we share God's love for them. At

other times, we may be able to present the gospel without having to cross barriers of need and circumstance.

4. Show the book *I Can Be a Mirror.* Explain that the purpose of the study is to examine the call to mission action and personal witnessing and to determine ways they can live out these tasks in the world around them.

5. Display the poster *Mission action: Ministering and witnessing to persons of special need and circumstance who are not members of the church or its programs; mission action is also combating social and moral problems.* Say: As we study the mission action section of the book, keep this definition in mind.

6. Chapter 1
   a) Present highlights of the content. Use a visual time line to illustrate the development of mission action from its beginning as a WMU task to the present. Use small posters clipped to string or taped to the wall to show the names and dates of each change.
   b) Ask: Who were your models of ministry? (p. 3)

7. Chapter 2
   a) Summarize the content by introducing each person described. Either ask persons in advance to portray them or enlist participants to represent them. During the presentation, ask participants to wear name tags and read a resume which you have prepared, using the information from this chapter.
   b) Ask for ideas on ways one person can do mission action.

8. Chapters 3, 4, 5, 6
   a) Divide your audience into four groups, one for each chapter. (One or two persons can do the assignment, or you may have more than one group for each chapter, depending on the size of your audience.)
   b) Assign each chapter to a group. For each chapter
      (1) identify the problem;
      (2) gather facts about the problem;
      (3) list ways suggested in the book for dealing with the problem;
      (4) list additional ways the group suggests.
   c) Ask groups to report.

9. Chapter 7
   a) Present highlights of the chapter.
   b) Divide the audience into two sections. Assign to one section the word *preventer,* and to the second section the word *corrector.* Ask each section to review the ideas for these two words and to brainstorm possible situations requiring each of these actions.
   c) Ask each group to report on their ideas.

10. Chapter 8
    a) Divide into groups to deal with the four topics beginning with the letter *A*.
    b) For each topic
       (1) define the problem;
       (2) gather the facts about the problem;
       (3) list ways suggested for dealing with the problem;
       (4) list other ways suggested by participants.
    c) Ask groups to report.
11. Review the poster defining *mission action*. Assign magazines and mission action materials to small groups to use in preparing a report on how each can be used in training for or doing mission action.
12. Display the poster *Personal witnessing: A Christian's sharing the gospel of Jesus Christ with another person and giving that person an opportunity to confess Jesus Christ as Saviour and Lord.* Say: Personal witnessing can take place when there is no barrier of special need or circumstance preventing an effective witness.
13. Chapter 9
    a) Review the highlights of the chapter using key words selected from the main ideas. Print the key words on small sheets of poster board with a felt-tip marker.
    b) Ask: Where and to whom may we witness?
14. Chapter 10
    a) Review highlights from the chapter.
    b) Read and discuss 1 Kings 19:15-21 and 2 Kings 2:1-14.
    c) Ask: Who have been your models for witnessing?
15. Chapter 11
    a) As you review the content of the chapter, discuss these questions as appropriate:
       (1) What kinds of busy-ness may keep us from witnessing?
       (2) How may we use our gifts in witnessing? (Read the Scripture passages listed on p. 57.)
       (3) What are hindrances to witnessing? Ask for suggestions beyond those listed in the chapter.
16. Chapter 12
    a) Ask someone to present a monologue telling the story of Bonnie Haight. Ask participants to analyze the story for Bonnie's feeling of need, and the various steps and persons involved in meeting that need with salvation.
    b) Ask for ideas on the various ways people are influenced to become Christians and how we can participate in that process.
17. Chapter 13
    a) Review the content. Use Luke 9 and 10 to trace the four steps in Jesus' plan of witnessing as described on page 63. Discuss how that applies to us today.

b) Present the four marks of a witness (p. 64) using these key words: *personally, verbally, confidence, and compassion.* Assign each word to a group for discussion and application.

18. Refer again to the personal witnessing poster. Reread the definition of *personal witnessing.* Distribute personal witnessing materials among the participants. Ask them to tell how that product may be used to train for or do personal witnessing.

Conclusion

Review the definitions of both *mission action* and *personal witnessing.* Ask if some will share some new insights and commitments to mission action and personal witnessing they have made as a result of this study. Close in prayer that each participant will seek and follow the leadership of the Holy Spirit in mission action and personal witnessing.

The Church Study Course

The Church Study Course is a Southern Baptist educational system consisting of more than 500 short courses for adults and youth combined with a credit and recognition system. Credit is awarded for each course completed. These credits may be applied to 1 or more of the 25 diplomas.

Complete details about the Church Study Course system, courses available, and diplomas offered may be found in a current copy of the *Church Study Course Catalog* and in the study course section of the *Church Materials Catalog.* The Church Study Course is sponsored by the Sunday School Board, Woman's Missionary Union, and the Brotherhood Commission.

Credit for the course (08129) may be obtained in two ways: (1) Read the book and participate in a 2½-hour study; (2) Read the book and complete all personal learning activities.

Credit for this course may apply toward the Woman's Missionary Union Leadership Diploma for WMU Officers, Baptist Women Officers, Baptist Young Women Officers, Acteens Leaders, Girls in Action Leaders, and Mission Friends Leaders.

Request credit on Form 725 "Church Study Course Enrollment/ Credit Request," available from Awards Office, Sunday School Board, 127 Ninth Avenue, North, Nashville, TN 37234.

A record of your awards will be maintained by the Awards Office. Twice each year copies will be sent to churches for distribution to members.

W883107•8M•0488